SIMON
WAS SAFE

A Passover Story

Exodus 7:19—12:42 FOR CHILDREN

Written by LaVonne Neff

Illustrated by Art Kirchhoff

COPYRIGHT © 1976 CONCORDIA PUBLISHING HOUSE, ST. LOUIS, MISSOURI

CONCORDIA PUBLISHING HOUSE LTD., LONDON, E. C. 1

MANUFACTURED IN THE UNITED STATES OF AMERICA

ALL RIGHTS RESERVED

ISBN 0-570-06104-0

Publishing House
St. Louis London

ARCH Books

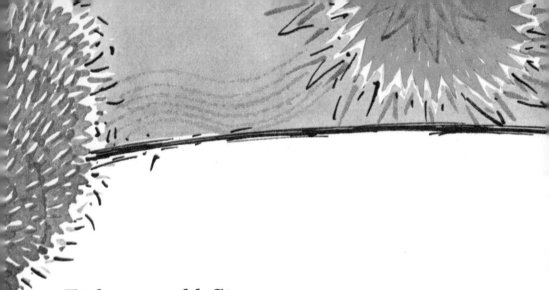

Eight-year-old Simon
Can run very fast.
He likes to climb trees and jump high.
But eight-year-old Simon's
Not playing today,
And if he weren't eight, he would cry.

Simon is sitting
Alone in his house.
His brothers are playing outside.
His parents are working
For Pharaoh the king;
They're looking for straw, far and wide.

Simon is scowling.
He's thinking quite hard
Of all that has happened of late.
Old Moses and Aaron,
King Pharaoh won't hear,
And now God has set a new date.

"At midnight tonight,"
God announced to the king,
"My angel will fly overhead.
And because of the way
You have hurt Israel,
He'll leave all your oldest boys dead!"

Simon's not big
Like his mom and his dad,
But he's bigger than Saul or Levi.
Simon's the firstborn
In his family,
And Simon's in no mood to die.

A noise near the door!
"Who's there?" Simon calls.
A tall form has blocked out the sun.
"Great-grandpa, my boy.
Why, you look pale as death!
You ought to be out having fun."

"Great-grandpa, at midnight,
Old Moses has said,
God is sending His angel of death.
And when he flies by,
The firstborn of man
And of beast are to draw their last breath!"

The old man nods wisely.
"I understand, Son —
But God doesn't want to hurt you.
When the sea turned to blood,
You had water to drink,
And tonight He'll watch over you, too.

"Remember when frogs
Ran all over the house?"
Simon laughs—one had jumped in his bed.
"They left Goshen-land
And ran straight for the king,
Who woke amidst heaps of them, dead.

"The lice didn't bite us.
The flies stayed away.
Our cattle and sheep stayed quite well.
We didn't get boils
(How the other folk scratched!)
And we hardly knew when the hail fell.

"While locusts ate their crops,
Our foodstuffs were sure.
While they cursed in the dark, we could see.
Whatever God's doing
To hurt Pharaoh's land,
He's doing so we can be free!"

"Great-grandpa," sighs Simon,
With tears in his eyes,
"Will we ever get out of this land?"
"Yes! Tonight," cries the old man.
"When Pharaoh's son dies,
God will lead us out by His own hand.

"Look! Here come your father,
Your mother, your aunt,
And your uncle—and what do they bring?
A basket of armbands,
Ten earrings of gold,
Precious stones, and a huge silver ring!"

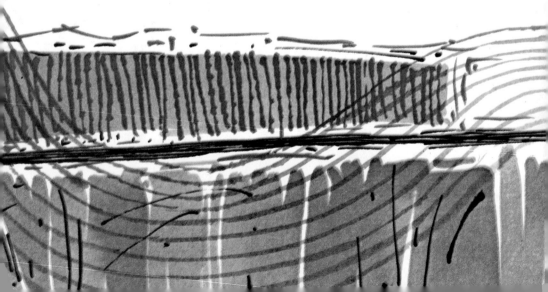

"Gifts from the Egyptians,"
His father explains.
"It is probably less than we're due,
After working for free
All these years. Simon, come.
We must . . . SIMON, I'M TALKING TO YOU."

The boy hangs his head.
"I was thinking, I guess. . . ."
"Well, stop thinking and work now, my son.
We must kill our best lamb,
Roast its flesh, paint our door
With its blood, and get ready to run."

Simon says softly,
"God's kept us from danger.
Great-grandpa says soon we'll go free.
Tonight, when the angel
Of death flies by Egypt—
Will anything happen to me?"

Father stops painting
The doorpost with blood.
"Tonight when the angel has flown,
The Egyptians will weep,
But my boy will be safe.
This blood takes the place of his own."

The family stands up
While they eat their best lamb,
Bitter herbs, and plain, unleavened bread.
Watching and praying,
At midnight they hear
The Egyptians bewailing their dead!

Mother gathers up dishes
And food for the trip.
Father takes all their clothes and his rod.
Simon steers Saul and Levi
To the group that's outside,
Getting ready to worship their God.

Eight-year-old Simon
Can win any race.
He can easily climb any tree.
And eight-year-old Simon
Is playing today —
God has saved him, and Simon is free!

DEAR PARENTS:

The story of Passover, especially as told from a child's point of view, is very frightening. We might well ask what this "miracle of death" means, especially for a child today.

Clearly, the story concerns freedom and captivity. The overarching theme is God's freeing the Israelites from their slavery to the Egyptians. But we also watch as 8-year-old Simon is freed from fear. At the beginning of the story Simon is, quite literally, frozen with fear. Gradually, through the help of his respected elders and God, he is liberated. By the end he can "win any race" and "climb any tree." This movement from stillness to activity parallels the Israelites' situation. And the source of Simon's fear, the angel of death, turns out to be the angel of life for both.

This might be a good time to talk to your child about fear and nightmares — how real they are, yet within the sheltering atmosphere of the Christian family and love, how inconsequential they become. Let your child describe real fears.

Finally, Jesus referred to Himself as the Passover Lamb. Simon's story is the Gospel story. Through Christ's sacrifice of Himself, the Lamb of God, we have been liberated from slavery to sin and death. Make sure your child understands that God has made it possible for all of us to live happily and freely — just like Simon.

THE EDITOR